Book of Rahim & Other Poems

Literary Activism

Series Editor: Amit Chaudhuri

Book of Rahim & Other Poems

Arvind Krishna Mehrotra

ashoka UNIVERSITY

CENTRE FOR The Creative and The Critical

First published by Westland Books, a division of Nasadiya Technologies Private Limited, in 2023

No. 269/2B, First Floor, 'Irai Arul', Vimalraj Street, Nethaji Nagar, Allappakkam Main Road, Maduravoyal, Chennai 600095

Westland and the Westland logo are the trademarks of Nasadiya Technologies Private Limited, or its affiliates.

ISBN: 9789357762991

10 9 8 7 6 5 4 3 2

Typeset by Jojy Philip, New Delhi 110 015

Printed at Thomson Press (India) Ltd

To the memory of my mother

Contents

A Note on the Series

'Literary activism' is a project that began in 2014 with a series of annual symposia. Its aim was to create a space for the kind of discussion on creativity no longer available in mainstream contexts (literary festivals, book launches) or in academic ones (conferences, classrooms, monographs). The literary activism website – literaryactivism.com – was created in 2020, and Centre for the Creative and the Critical at Ashoka University came into existence in 2022 at Ashoka University to give this project a home, and to look at the kind of thinking that writing and the arts comprise.

This new imprint, 'literary activism', is meant to carry forward these ambitions in the realm of publishing. The art vs science debate is now a historical relic, but what interests us is the possibility of creating a meaning for writing that's separate from market value and academic legitimacy. And we wish to recall that art and writing are not synonymous with the generalised academic discipline called the 'humanities': they have an angularity to it, and to the social science perspectives the humanities are now subsumed under. The 'literary activism' imprint wishes not only to publish good writing, but to pursue this angularity.

I

BOOK OF RAHIM

Abd al-Rahim Khan-i-Khanan (1556–1627), a Baharlu Turk, was an important figure in the Mughal nobility during the reigns of Akbar and Jehangir. A poet, translator, and military general who led successful imperial campaigns and was bestowed with many honours, he was proficient in Chagatay Turkic, Persian, Arabic, and Braj, had some knowledge of Sanskrit, and even picked up a smattering of Portuguese at Akbar's suggestion, which enabled him to converse with traders and Jesuits. Described as 'a man of the sword as well as of the pen', he was also known for his munificence.

Indian children read Rahim's *dohas* (rhyming couplets), of which he wrote some 300, in their Hindi textbooks in school. Little is told of his life or, if told, is remembered, but the *dohas*, once memorised, are seldom forgotten. Unless his name appears in it, and sometimes it does not, you might recall the couplet and not know it is Rahim's. It has passed into the language.

A Trooper in Ahmedabad
1583

When Gujrat was finally conquered, M. Khan Khanan gave his whole property to his soldiers...
—*Ain-i-Akbari*, vol 1, tr. Blochmann

Outnumbered four to one,
advised to hold back
till reinforcements arrived,
he rushed into battle
at Sarkhej,
surprising the enemy.
Afterwards, surprising us

by giving away
every scrap he owned.
I was the last to show up,
come for my share
when he had nothing left
to give. Of what use
an inkstand to a trooper?

Mulla Muhammad Amin Khurasani

Burhanpur, 1615

I do not
understand what is written in these pages
or the script
in which they're written.

I bind
as the calligrapher copies.
He reads the words,
I the paper, the size, the inks.

An expert in the art of paper marbling and a renowned bookbinder and illuminator, Khurasani was employed in Abd al-Rahim's Burhanpur library, one of the great private libraries of the Mughal period. It had books in diverse languages.

Who Were These People

Burhanpur, 1615

Who were these people,
where have they gone,
the calligraphers,

papermakers,
bookbinders,
and illuminators,

the gilders and architects
who made this the Iran
of the Deccan?

Where are the shops
they bought the colours from,
the nibs and brushes?

Where are the workshops,
the floor desks,
the mats they sat on?

Where are their shoes
outside the door?
Where's the door?

Passing through
the Ruby Garden,
they'd have stopped

by the lotus pond,
square as a chess board,
surrounded with trees,

and looked at themselves
in the rippled mirror.
Where have they all gone?

No likenesses survive,
and what if they had?
They looked like you and me.

They were you and me.

Abd al-Rahim's Burhanpur library is said to have had a staff of ninety-five working in different capacities and about a hundred daily visitors.

Schoolboy's Rahim

He outlived his four sons. One died of drink.
One's head was cut off and delivered,
wrapped in cloth, as a gift. One died young.
When his favourite son died none dared tell him.

No mausoleum covers their graves.
The tomb with blue tiles on the dome
was built for Miyan Fahim, his faithful servant
born of a slave girl.

Keep grief
to yourself, Rahim says.
        Sharing doesn't help.

It only leaves
chinks in your armour
        that others exploit.

We read him in school. The alphabet was familiar,
but you scrunched up the eyes to read the page.
The meaning had to be cribbed. Hindi was grief,
and grief the sports field if you missed a sitter.

Rahim: *Dohas*

Don't break
the thread of love,
        Rahim says.

Broken, it cannot be
fixed. Fixed,
        the knot shows.

*

They look
like twins,
koel and crow,
until you hear
        their call.

Come spring, Rahim says,
and you know
        which is which.

*

Seeing greatness,
don't think yourself
        small.

A needle does
what a sword
        cannot.

*

Drop the small-minded
as you would a piece of coal.
Hot, it burns the hand.
Cold, it blackens it.

*

Blessed are those
for whom benevolence is a habit.

When you give henna,
Rahim says,

your own hands turn
the henna's colour.

*

Don't utter a word.
Watch the days
    spin by.

When the good days come,
Rahim says, things change
    quickly.

*

Once in a while
it's good to be
in a spot
    of trouble.

You know
who is with you
    and who's not.

*

When things go wrong
they keep going wrong.

When milk spoils, Rahim says,
no amount of churning

will turn it
into butter.

*

Pearls get their lustre from it,
dough its give,
it has the gift of humility.

Never leave home
without water,
        Rahim says.

*

Leave it alone, Rahim says.
The body's all right
        the way it is.

The earth too suffers
cold, heat, rain.

*

You slice off the head
and rub salt in the cucumber
to rid it of bitterness.

The person who speaks
bitter words, Rahim says,
deserves no better.

*

What if you are
the tallest of men
and like the date palm.

It gives no shade to birds
and the fruit's out of reach.

*

If the rosary's broken,
you thread the beads again,
and you thread them a hundred times.

You do the same, Rahim says,
with someone you love.

*

Bad company
surrounds you.

It depends
on who you are.

To the sandalwood tree, Rahim says,
the snakes coiled round it

make no difference.

*

Aim at one target
and you hit the others.

Aim at several
and you hit none.

Water the root, Rahim says.
You don't water each fruit

separately.

*

It's the rainy season, Rahim says,
and the koel is quiet.

Everywhere the sound
of toads croaking.

Who'll listen to me,
it thinks?

*

The tears
that flow out of your eyes
reveal your grief,
Rahim says,

just as someone
who is thrown
out of the house
reveals your secrets.

*

The elderly
should forgive.

Kids will be kids.

Does God
diminish,
asks Rahim,

if an ant
kicks it?

*

To walk the path of love, Rahim says,
is to ride a wax horse over fire.

*

Stay away
from nasty men.

Their friendship's as bad
as their enmity,

just as a dog's lick is as unwelcome
as its bite.

*

Once lit, it
burns out.
Once it burns out,
it cannot be
        relit.

Unlike the fire
of love, Rahim says,
that revives
even as it
        fades.

*

Take fish
out of water
and it dies.

Shake a bee
out of a flower
and it settles on

the next one.

*

Your worries,
Rahim says,
you best keep
        to yourself.

People will listen,
ears cocked.
        None can share them.

*

Well-being, upbringing, a cough,
happiness, enmity, alcoholism, and love:

They cannot be hidden, Rahim says,
even if you tried.

*

The tree does not eat
the fruit it bears

nor the lake drink
its water:

The good give away their wealth
for the same reason,

Rahim says.

*

The fate of an oil lamp,
Rahim says,
is the fate of a son

who brings dishonour.
There's light at first,
and after a while, darkness.

*

The mind, pearls, flowers, milk, and fruit juices
are good while they are good.

Once they spoil,
a thousand tricks won't save them.

*

When desires cease, worries cease,
and the mind can do as it pleases.

Once you want nothing,
you're the King of Kings.

*

The person's dignity,
the regard you have,
the affection in your eyes,

nothing is left of them,
Rahim says,

the minute you ask
a favour.

*

The rumble of October clouds, empty of rain:
The nostalgic talk, Rahim says, of the once rich.

*

He's come to pluck flowers.
It's our turn tomorrow,
the buds say,
seeing the gardener arrive.

*

Imagine a paper kite
climbing
the sky of love.

The face is distant,
Rahim says,
till the mind reels it back
to where the heart is.

*

Without learning, without intelligence,
without faith, fame, or benevolence,
you're no better than
an animal without tail or horn.
Why do you walk on two legs at all?
Rahim says.

*

Better, Rahim says,
to live in the forest
and enjoy wild fruit

than at a family gathering
be the poor relative.

*

The eight watches of the day,
Rahim says, beat a single drum:
You are not here for long.

*

II

GHALIB, A DIARY

DELHI 1857–1858

Note

Ghalib wrote the *Dastanbūy* (Nosegay) between May 1857 and September 1858, in the form of a diary narrating the events of the Sepoy Mutiny of 1857. It is his formal petition to Queen Victoria for the restoration of his pension that had been stopped by the East India Company.

Given his military-aristocratic background, and seeing the destruction they had wrought on Delhi, Ghalib could barely hide his contempt for the rebels. At the same time, since this was a petition to the Queen, he could not afford openly to be critical of the British. His relations with them were already difficult because of his association with the Mughal court, which he frequently attended. Though his mad brother was killed by a British soldier, Ghalib conceals this fact in the diary, saying, instead, that his brother died after five days of fever. The actual cause of death we know from another account.

Professor Khwaja Ahmed Faruqi's 1971 translation from the original Persian is the basis of 'Ghalib, A Diary'—its incidents, details, often its very words are drawn from that translation. My other debt, broadly speaking, is to Basil Bunting's 'Chomei at Toyama', which provided me with the form, the rhythmic pace, the inspiration to condense a prose work into verse. Like Chomei's, Ghalib's tone is elegiac; like Chomei, Ghalib belonged to the 'minor nobility'. There are also, between the two works, profound differences. The communal divide, mentioned matter-of-factly in *Dastanbūy*, is entirely absent from Bunting's poem, as is colonial rule. It's not too much of a stretch to say that the poem has four authors: Ghalib, Faruqi, Bunting, and myself; though my job, as far as I can see, has been to stir the mix and serve, adding a few ingredients of my own. Ultimately, origins, ours, a poem's, are, mostly, labours of love. And, like love, they are mysterious, unfathomable.

Dehra Dun
15 September 2021

Without indulging in ornament we can say simply that the times have changed.
—Mirza Ghalib, *Dastanbūy*, tr. Khwaja Ahmad Faruqi

That winter my fuel was the walls of my own house.
—Basil Bunting, 'Chomei at Toyama'

I come from Samarkand,
where, as everywhere,
once blood had been shed,
you bled into each other,

never to touch the soil
the grandmothers
came from for they came
from somewhere else again.

We are the flower
of roots we don't know,
the roots whose flower
we don't know.

We only see one side
of the moon,
one side of the word,
one side of our flower-like

moon-like faces.

Except that there were no fountains
and Catherine wheels to slow
their advance through the countryside,
units of rebel sepoys,
like wedding processions
arriving from different directions,
entered the city gates, triumphant.
They bowed their peasant heads
on the royal threshold
and stood around gawking at the lights.

Among them: tax evaders,
conmen, embezzlers, thugs.
Set free by the rebels
before they started for Delhi,
they came looking for governorships.
Cut-throats allowed into the royal presence
is part of the strangeness of the times.

His far-flung provinces shrunk
to the street in the window,
the hawker's cries within earshot,
the Mughal emperor
was a waning moon
yet his light was eclipsed.

In the hall of private audience
I'd sit with him twice a week,
blue pencil in hand,
going over his ghazals,
measuring line lengths.
It's what I lived on
till the money ran out.

If he was busy,
I'd wait and go home.
To look at his large eyes
was to lift the veil
on three hundred years of sadness.
It's what you're left with in the end,
the vacancy of grief.

I heard shouts outside.
The British agent has been murdered.
The killings had started, the looting.
Our reputations meant a cipher to them.
Men who couldn't tell an arrow from an axe
begged for their lives as if lives mattered.
Those who knew where the wealth was buried
turned against their masters.
Rough labourers who shovelled mud had found in it pieces of gold.
One whose mother borrowed fire to light her brick stove
proclaimed himself sovereign of fire.
One whose father wandered dust-stained through the village
proclaimed himself ruler of the wind.
Slim-waisted women whose bodies had glittered like raw silver
walked barefoot.
The sepoys slept on the silken beds
they were recruited to guard.

No blade of grass can stop the flow of running water.

The fires from rooftops
outshone the morning sun.
It seemed the havelis of Balli Maran
were self-combusting.
Their walls curved in the wind
and collapsed like tent cloth
without a murmur.

If music is a free gift
from the home of a neighbour,
welcome, too, the ashes.
I slapped my white muslin tunic
that was flecked with grey
and saw it turn black.

None cried for help.
Not that there were none to help,
there was none left to cry.

> *From under the earth only spring returns,*
> *while we again and again turn to dust.*

I had cat visitors.
They're the first to hear the news.

The eyes are not lifeless cracks in a wall
but will weep at India's desolation.

Except for a ridge at the western edge
where they're barricaded, the British,
those possessors of knowledge and wisdom,
control no ground. They'd been taken by surprise.
Sa'di of Shiraz said

> *The slave must bow his head before the master.*
> *The ball has no choice but to follow the swing of the mallet.*

The ball had changed course.
Disobedience to the ruler is disobedience to the Lord.

When their vengeful guns fired,
it was sepoy against sepoy,
rebels against their kin,

both drawn from the same pool of rustics,
one true to their salt and the other
who betrayed it.
They were evenly matched.
Destruction such as I've not known.

The months of May and June
and the sun has entered Gemini.
Clouds of dust rise in the heat.
The air sizzles. Not a leaf stirs.
There was once a city called Delhi.
Between millstones it was crushed.
The plunder never stopped, the killings.
You can run out of nib pens and ink,
not weapons.
A whole armoury can walk on two legs,
and then there are bare hands.
There's fire in the heart
and never enough to melt it.

The rebels had entered the city
on a Monday. On a Monday,
after four months and four days,
on fourteenth September
eighteen hundred and fifty-seven,
the city was retaken.
It's as if everything had happened
in the same twenty-four hours.
In each lane the same calamity;
in each lane a different one.
A general massacre was declared.
The citizens were asked to leave.

On hearing a commotion –
the firing, the noise –
my brother Mirza Yusuf Khan stepped out
to see what was going on
and was shot dead by the soldiers.
He was my age; we were close.
He had been mad for half his life
and went around naked.
His wife and children had left him by then.

Whether coarse or fine,
we could not leave the house
to buy cloth for the shroud.
There was no water
to wipe the dead man's face
with a kerchief,
none to bathe the body,
no graveyard nearby to bury him,
no bricks and mortar to mark the spot.
Seeing my plight, neighbours
asked me for some white sheets,
dug a grave in an adjoining mosque,
put the body in the pit and returned.
The Hindus are more fortunate.
They can carry their dead to the river
and burn them or bury them
in shallow graves in the sand.

Even in a time of retribution, some will be kind.
A raised British sword, I've heard it said,
would spare an innocent at the last minute.

A man's character isn't always reflected in his buttons.

Along roadsides, rebel corpses were stacked like firewood.
Some toppled over.
You watched your step when you passed them,
the road could be slippery, and you held your nose.
Cries of suffocation filled jail cells.
Human flesh poured out from cannon mouths.
Men hung limp from gibbets.

The lock on the door or the lack of a door,
the walls green with vegetation as if made of grass,
tell of houses whose owners have fled
to the tombs on the outskirts
or to hamlets further away.
Among them Amin-ud-din Khan Bahadur
and Muhammad Ziya-ud-din Khan Bahadur,
who in order to uphold their dignity
set out for the pargana of Loharu
with their wives, children, servants,
three elephants, and forty horses.
Besieged by the plundering soldiers
during the halt at Mehrauli,
they were left with only the clothes on their backs
and the elephants that stood there
like three great burnt-out silos.

Those who're in hiding have no way of knowing
whether those who stayed behind are alive.

Living can kill anyone,
it never reveals its ways,
for then came famine, cholera, fever.
I ran out of money
and sold my possessions.
My clothes and bedding were all that was left.
I sold them one by one.

While others ate bread, I ate trousers.
I'm sixty-three.

With stones we blocked up the gate to our lane
and in my empty house I sought
a place to hide.
We could not get to the well
and doused our fire with brackish water.
Another name for this fire is thirst.
When it rained
we tied up a sheet in the courtyard
and placed jars beneath it to collect the drops.

> *O Ghalib, when He seems to fail most, our Heavenly Friend*
> *comes to our aid in ways we do not understand.*

It's hard to live without servants
and mine looked to me for help,
their voices as painful to me
as the untimely crowing of a cock.
The washerman and barber,
who came on fixed days of the week,
haven't been seen in a year.

Of Muslims there are fewer than a thousand
remaining in Delhi.
I'm one of them,
an irreligious half Muslim.
I cannot do without drink
but don't touch pork.

One day around noon
white soldiers scaled the wall
near the gate, climbed over the rooftops,
and jumped down into the street.

Ignoring the smaller houses
they came directly to mine
and took me, my two adopted children,
my servants, and a few neighbours
for questioning. Colonel Burn was polite.
He only asked me my name and let me go.
The others he asked their professions.

Mohammedan has become another word for rebel.
The Hindus have started trickling back.
The dog of suspicion does not follow them.

I've only written
of what I've heard
and a little of what I've seen.
Of the emperor's trial,
his sons' execution,
I've said nothing.
The treasure of my writing
comes from what I hear
and there's much to hear still.
I need to hear more to say more,
listen to what's being said
at streetcorners. My ears beg for alms
from the tongues of the people.
Not everything said is counterfeit.

Except the one time
the soldiers came to take me,
I haven't set foot
on the threshold, walked
into the lane or bazaar.
The outside world is
confined to the expanse of sky
above my courtyard.

The diary is sketchy.
I'm aware of the gaps.
The sequence of events
may have been disarranged.

Friends made copies of my Urdu verses,
I never kept any.
Now that I craved for them,
nothing remained of their libraries.

Charred windows stared at you
like wide open eyes.
There were pictures from China
on the walls.

I'd lie awake at night,
no oil in the lamp,
waiting for a flash of lightning
to look for the water jug.

Thorns surround me
from every side.
They're in my path when I go out,
and stick to my clothes when I return.

It is not necessary
to record their names, but the four
who helped me through these
difficult times were

Mahesh Das,
bounteous as the river,
who quenched my thirst
when I could ill afford foreign wine;

Hira Singh,
one of my pupils,
faithful, young,
ever conscious of his duties;

Shivji Ram Brahman,
who seldom leaves
this sorrowing dervish alone
and is blessed with a courteous son;

and Har Gopal 'Tafta',
the sweet-tongued poet
who regularly sends letters
and ghazals from Meerut.

There's one song to sing,
though we all sing it differently.
There's one life to live, whose
unreceding end we don't see.

My petitions that my title, robe of honour,
and pension be restored have been returned.
The note from the administrator said
they weren't submitted through proper channels.
I'm told this is an encouraging sign.
At least there's someone paying attention.
The rest of my time goes in writing letters.
My pen crawls at the speed of a half-dead ant.
Money for postage is hard to come by.
Afterwards I worry if the letter will reach.
The hum of telegraph wires
is good only for short messages.

III

BOOK OF LAHORE

to the memory of
Begum Badar Hasan of Panipat
and Amolak Ram Mehta of Lahore

Lahore

Unterrestrial, ungoogleable, unreachable,
landlocked city that erupts from the sea
and disappears in the sky;
whose birds sing in the dawn to come;
the walled city without walls, Lahore.

Behind razor wire, the home town
next door, the Temple Road address
to which I cannot ask my way back;
the city of a thousand names and one:
it can only be Lahore.

Men of the hinterland arrived at its gates,
slow moving men with keen eyes bringing bales
of cloth, marking the doors to knock on. They knew
their sums and flourished as seeds do
when the ground is virgin, waiting to be clothed.

Then when nations rose like party balloons in the sky
to be sold by balloon men at streetcorners, they melted
into trains. Their houses stand, their names
still on gateposts, they themselves dead. Asked
for the blood group, I extend a finger called Lahore.

11 Temple Road

On the Temple Road land, Daddyji built a house, which was three stories high and was made of bricks and cement.
—Ved Mehta, *Daddyji* (1972)

I had always known of 11 Temple Road. My mother, who was the eldest of Daddyji's seven children, never spoke about it, never described it, and I didn't ask. All I knew was that I was born in that house at a time of suspicion, rumour, fear, stabbings, and riots. 'On April 16,' Ved wrote in *Face to Face* (1957), his first book, 'a child was born to Pom, a fine, healthy boy. Yet the times had their due, for no festivity, no celebration greeted him, even though he was the first grandson.' There is in *The Ledge Between the Streams* (1982), a subsequent volume of Ved's autobiography, a graphic account of the same event, and it is similar to what my 94-year-old aunt, my mother's only surviving sibling, told me the other day when I asked her what she recalled of my birth. 'You were born in the side room that opened onto the veranda,' she said. 'It was Daddyji's study. You were premature and Daddyji had to rush out in his car to get Dr Ansuiya Bhagat who did the delivery. You had no heartbeat and weren't breathing. She gave an injection straight into your heart before we heard your first cry. At night we heard shouts of "Allahu Akbar". We could see the fires from the roof. Your mother feared for your life and even thought of sending you away with a close friend of the family. He lived in an area that was thought to be safer than ours.'

On a visit to San Francisco I was introduced to the writer and librarian Moazzam Sheikh. He is from Lahore. On his next trip there, he said, he'd go to Temple Road and tell me about it. He spoke of the city's Punjabi writers and mentioned some names. A few months after we met I received an email from him:

> I was in Lahore in July, and one day my wife, my sister-in-law and I managed to drive to Temple Road (under life threatening heat). It was a tough task as the faces of some of the houses had withered or altered or converted into commercial buildings, but we tried our best. Still we couldn't pin down what might have been 11 Temple Road.
>
> Then out of curiosity, my sister-in-law entered a by-lane and realized the alley too was part of Temple Road and there we saw the house you were born in. We took photos of the neighbouring houses as well. The marble plaque on the side of the gate came out blurry but it has a 'Hindu' name still. I vaguely remember the last name was Mehta. I will ask my sister-in-law to visit the house again when the temperatures are cooler and take a photo of the marble plate with the name on it. I wish you can visit Lahore sometime in the near future.

The by-lane that was part of Temple Road would have been 'Mehta *Gullie*', which is a chapter title in *Face to Face*:

> ... The Mehta *Gullie*, or street, was separated from the main house by a five-foot wall.
>
> Climbing this wall, we would find ourselves in a completely different world, for behind it and within a radius of two city blocks lay the houses of all the Mehta families, comprising a clan of some fifty persons. These houses opened on the *gullie*, which was off the Temple Road and formed a square. Our house was not included in the square, since it had been built before the planning of the Mehta *Gullie*, but it was only a block away.

Moazzam sent the photos with the email, including the one of the 'blurry' Mehta name on the gatepost. But, for me, the house still remained a blur, both architecturally and emotionally.

In 2012, three years before I met Moazzam, my mother had fallen on the veranda of our house in Dehra Dun—the one she had brought me to from Lahore when I was four weeks old—and broken her femur. With the help of a walker she was able to move around again but it wasn't the same. I'd give her the newspaper to read with her

11 Temple Road, Lahore. I was born in the front room on the right of the veranda. Photo courtesy Aleesha Hamid

morning tea, even though I knew she could not follow what she was reading. There were times when it felt she was losing her memory. I became preoccupied with other things and forgot about Temple Road. The past can disappear quickly. It can, as I was to learn later, just as quickly return.

*

On 29 July 1993, on a visit to Lahore, Adil Jussawalla went looking for the past in the same area and for the same reason, to locate 'an ancestral house'. He bought a pair of pathanis at English Shoes and casually made an enquiry of the middle-aged salesman if he knew about a house in Temple Road where the Jussawallas once lived. The salesman looked at the customer with wide-open eyes. The Jussawallas, he said, were very well-known and the house must still be there. 'It may have been, it may still be, but I never found it,' Adil says in 'A Place in the Sun', the essay on his father I'm paraphrasing from. His father, Jehangir, had spent part of his childhood in Temple Road. 'He couldn't remember the number of the house; no one, to this day, can tell me. He, his mother and his three brothers left that house in 1914 and settled in Poona.' His father was seven years old at the time.

*

I got to know Anjum Altaf through his book *Transgressions: Poems Inspired by Faiz Ahmed Faiz* (2019). He lives in Lahore and before long I found myself telling him about 11 Temple Road. One day he sent me a link. Somewhat to my disbelief, it was the review of an art exhibition *Imagined Archives – Residual and Remembrance* that had been held there. A search turned up more reviews, one of them by Zohreen Murtaza of The Karachi Collective. Through their website I contacted Fatma Shah, the exhibition's curator, and learnt about the subsequent history of the house that Daddyji built.

After the family of Amolak Ram Mehta moved out, that of Begum Badar Hasan, to whom the house had been allotted, moved in. She came from a prominent Shia family of Panipat. The poet Altaf Hussain Hali, who was Ghalib's disciple and first biographer, was a relative. Fatma is married to Abbas Hasan, Begum Badar Hasan's youngest grandson. It was during the 2020 lockdown, Fatma wrote me in an email, that she had 'the idea of reopening the family home'. It had not been lived in since 2005. Something that also made her think of reopening it, and ways to reopen it, was the death the same year of her husband's uncle, the engineer, politician, and bird watcher Mubashir Hasan.

The idea, that she had till then only been dreaming about, now became something more specific: 'an excavation of history and collective memories associated with the residents of the house and Lahore.' Her quest, she said, 'began while reorganising the family's present library, and I came across a book, signed by "Raj Kanwar Mehta, B.A. Class, Govt College, Lahore", and began thinking about lives interrupted in 1947 & families displaced.' The book was *Mount Helicon: A School Anthology of Verse* and bore the stamp of the 'Mehta Home Library Lahore'. On the title page was the first stanza of R.L. Stevenson's 'Bright is the ring of words'.

More things surfaced: a hand-crank ice cream maker; a drum of galvanized tin with a lid and stand, used for storing water; a wooden chest. In a separate email to Ved's wife Linn Cary she wrote:

Photo courtesy Moazzam Sheikh

> We'd love to pass on the few objects that we have now noticed in the house, most significantly two large metal serving platters or *thaali*, with [Ved's] father's initials. The gate still says Amolak Ram Mehta—as really nobody ever felt the need to erase history, is my guess.

Apart from the undying objects of daily use, the two displaced families, the Hasans and the Mehtas, had left behind in Panipat and Lahore a shared past that went back several centuries. They could easily have passed off for each other. Unbeknownst to them, what lay in the future for the families was not without common threads. 'It is almost uncanny', Fatma wrote to Linn

> that Dr Amolak Ram Mehta and my father-in-law Dr Shubbar Hasan (Mubashir's elder brother) would have an almost identical career path. He also qualified as a doctor from King Edward's Medical College, though much later (around 1942) and after his post grad work in the UK and the US worked with the public health department in Punjab to build the infrastructure for the control of infectious diseases especially tuberculosis in Pakistan!

Though I could not put a face to it, the name Raj Kanwar sounded familiar. Once again I opened *Daddyji* as I would an encyclopaedia. He turned out to be Daddyji's younger brother. 'Raj Kanwar', Ved writes, 'passed his B.A. on the second try. He came to Daddyji with the good news, and said, "I want to join the police."'

Fatma Shah's *Imagined Archives* exhibition was dedicated to Ved and Mubashir Hasan.

The photo of the gatepost that Moazzam had sent showed not only the 'blurry' name but also the rust-coloured hinged gate. On both its leaves was a bright blue signboard that read

PAKISTAN INDIA
PEOPLES' FORUM FOR
PEACE & DEMOCRACY
11 TEMPLE ROAD LHR
Pakistan Secretariat

Between the first two words, PAKISTAN and INDIA, the signboard painter had squeezed in a dove carrying an olive branch in its beak. The board has since been removed. In some recent photos that Anjum Altaf sent, I spotted it leaning forlornly against an inside wall. One of the founders of the Peoples' Forum in 1994 was Mubashir Hasan.

*

My mother's bedroom had always been sparsely furnished. It had a Godrej steel almirah with a mirror, a bed, and a built-in cupboard with three shelves. The bulb socket inside the cupboard held a 10-watt bulb that was used as a night light. The switch malfunctioned. For cheerfulness, there was a framed picture that Daddyji had gifted her. I had seen the same print in his house in Delhi. He would have picked it up on one of his visits to Germany in the 1950s. I have never looked at the print in any detail, though it now hangs above my bed as it did above my mother's. I moved into her room after her death. Most likely it is a Renaissance Madonna and Child.

In the cupboard my mother kept her puja things, not that she was religious. She never visited temples, prayed to no gods. I have an early memory of waiting for her to return from the Cosmopolitan Club. She played rummy, but played the harmonium just as enthusiastically and led the bhajan singing. In winter a ball of wool would follow her around as though it had been trained to do so. She liked putting the cable design in the pullovers she knitted. My mother's puja things consisted of a joss-stick holder, a packet of joss sticks, and a box of matches. There was a souvenir shop terracotta replica of a temple, though it may well have been of a palace in Rajasthan. In a stainless steel *thaali* were prayer beads, a bell with a long handle, toy-sized brass utensils that I never saw her touch, and a creepy looking seashell with my father's name painted on it in red and green. The shell would have been presented to him when he retired from the Bhilai Steel Plant. One of its spikes had since broken. There was a framed photograph of her guru under whose spell she had come in her middle age, the frame propped against the back wall. A photograph of the guru's wife was in an adjoining frame. The photographs, too, were souvenirs but given to my parents rather than bought. The guru family had its ashram in Jabalpur and its prime disciple, Brijmohini Sarin, had set up an ashram of her own in Deep Mandap, Agra Road, Mulund, Bombay. It's where I lived for the two years—1966 to 1968—that I was studying for my MA degree and brought out the mimeographed magazines *ezra* and *fakir*. It was around then that I got to know Adil and Arun Kolatkar.

The cupboard, though quite empty, looked crowded. On one shelf was a rectangular Kashmiri box. Made of walnut wood and intricately carved, I'd never shown any interest in it till I noticed there was a termite gallery along one side. When I lifted the lid I found the box was full of white ants. While they had left the box reasonably intact, the termites, barring one or two things, had almost completely destroyed its contents: documents, letters, cards, horoscopes. I saved what papers I could and put them out in the sun, as though they were wet pieces of cloth. Looking at the condition they were in, many of them did not seem worth keeping but I could not throw them away either. They were my mother's memorabilia. She was then still alive.

Of one document I could not make out more than a few incomplete words: 'de', 'more', 'ent', 'ore'. It was like looking at a papyrus fragment or hearing my mother's incoherent speech, the half erased words in her mouth that she was trying to make whole, give communicative shape to. She died last year and how quickly I've forgotten the period when she was in decline. I had forgotten her attempts at speaking, though to herself she would have thought that her speech was as clear and authoritarian as it had always been. I would pat her cheek as though to tell her that I understood everything that she said. With the help of a search engine I figured out the words in the document. It was my father's bachelor's degree from de Montmorency Dental College, Lahore.

*

Till the other day Lahore had been barren of memories. 'I wish you can visit Lahore...' Moazzam had written. More than this, my wish now is to live out my years in the city of my birth, a birth I had not thought about until now, never imagining that it had anything to do with me. One is born. Big deal. I used to collect stamps and my album has pages for Andorra, Danzig, and Tannou Touva. Another album, my father's, has more pages for Indian Native States—starting with Alwar and Bamra and ending with Travancore and Wadhwan—than for the United States. Countries keep disappearing off the face of the map or changing their shapes or their names, but a piece of land remains where it's always been, fixed in geography if not in history and schoolboy stamp albums. Perhaps this is why Indians, when they return from abroad, make the gesture of bending and touching the soil, then bringing their fingers to their foreheads. It is not, as they believe, the soil of a country that they touch but, symbolically, they are kissing the earth. They have returned home.

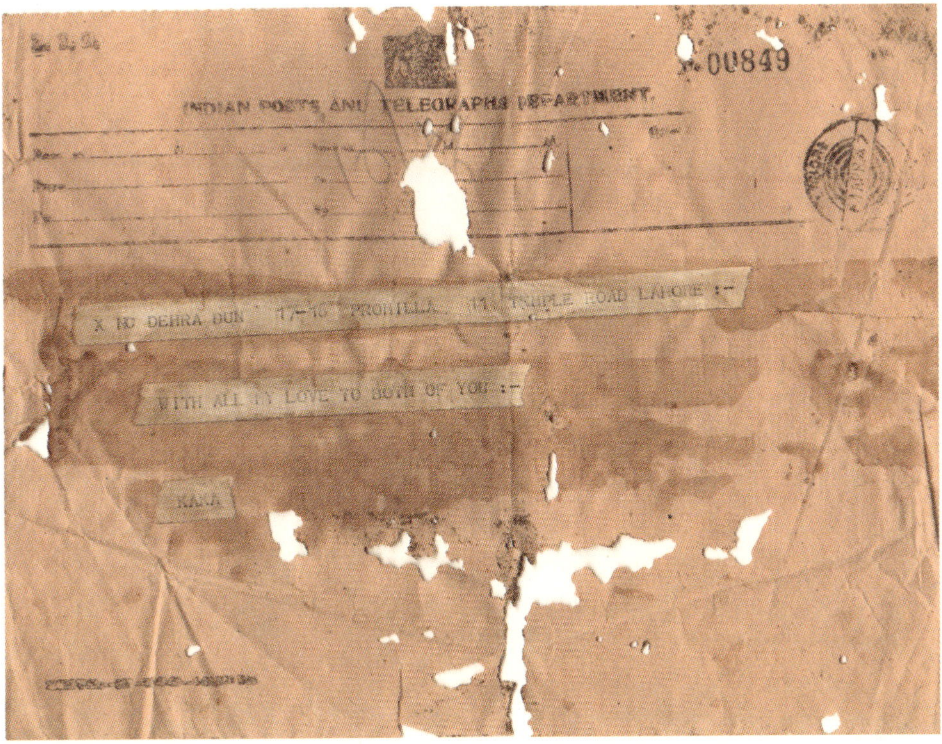

00849

INDIAN POSTS AND TELEGRAPHS DEPARTMENT.

X NC DEHRA DUN 17-10 PROMILLA 11 TEMPLE ROAD LAHORE :-

WITH ALL MY LOVE TO BOTH OF YOU :-

KAKA

Congratulatory telegram sent to 11 Temple Road, Lahore, at the time of my birth, by my father (Kaka) in Dehra Dun.

'Caught up in someone else's story'

Caught up in someone else's
story, fleeing in opposite
directions by rail or road
across a line drawn to meet a deadline,

were two families. One of them,
in haste, had abandoned a house
of many thresholds, as had the one
that arrived to live in it.

Unknown to each other,
joined by walls that divided them,
they had utensils in common,
clothes, an idiom, an address.

Memories dry up like short
streams, fill up like trenches,
or are demolished, and history
is easier said than undone.

'Doors have ears'

Doors have ears
but also mouths,
eyes that see everything.
This one, a screen door,
opens onto a wide

veranda. If you had eyes
you'd see it smiling
as it watches us
from a bay window
we look out of.

‘Whatever became’

Whatever became
of Raj Kanwar Mehta
of Government College?

He left behind a book,
that did better than him.
He inscribed his name

on the flyleaf,
which is where he survives,
remembered by someone

who never knew
Raj Kanwar Mehta.

‘Kept in a kitchen basket by the window’

Kept in a kitchen basket by the window,
a few loose papers damaged by white ants,
the holes, brown at the edges, like small
or large islands seen from an airplane.
Among them, her matriculation certificate;
her wedding invitation;
an Eid card, a minaret in the background,
a woman’s hands lifted in prayer, the face European;
a horoscope, the colour of the inks unfaded;
a handwritten note from her teacher
at Presentation Convent, Rawalpindi;
and congratulatory telegrams
sent to Lahore when I was born.
Undecided whether to bin the papers or keep them,
I leave them where they are – my mother’s ashes.

IV

LAUGH CLUB OF GANDHI PARK

Neighbourhood

Faces

A thought is born
like a bird inside you
and its shadow
hops across your face.
        We can read

the fledgling.
But with those
whose posters hang
from every lamp post
        there's no such thing.

Under their unbreathing
skins they wear
a mask of papier-mâché,
struck off a mould
        and affixed to torsos

when they stand
before a cheering crowd
of flag wavers
who've walked long distances
        to attend the rally:

among them, faces
like blown roofs, like mudslides,
like thumbprints. They
listen. The great hero winks,
    and from his

well-cushioned mouth
there issues forth
a stream of colour schemed thoughts:
his tips to the poor
    for living.

After Mangalesh Dabral

General Post Office

Weightless himself,
    he sat by the road outside
the general post office
    with a weighing scale.

I stepped on it
    cautiously. He peered
into the analog display
    and waited. I weigh fifty-six kilos.

As I paid him
    I noticed
his eyelashes were whiter
    than his skull cap.

Bengali Library Lane

A brown muffler
        covering his head and mouth,
you could not make him out
        in the uninhabited dark
of the one-room grocery store
        from which winter light
slanted away. In the entrance,
        blocking it, was a metal rack
that held small bottles
        of cold-pressed mustard oil.
Do you read Bengali?
        I asked him.
I've forgotten the alphabet,
        he replied, though I'd learnt it
as a child, but I know someone
        who can help you.
Let me give you his address.
        You go meet him.
He doesn't live in this locality.
        There's no one here,
in Bengali Library Lane,
        who reads Bengali.

Beni Bazaar

His is the last remaining shop
in Beni Bazaar. Sitting by himself
under a row of grandfather clocks,
he's looking at the road that has no
traffic. Pull up a chair, he says,
seeing me come in.
I need to change the button cell,
I tell him, unbuckling my watch.
He opens the back case
with a pair of blunt tweezers
meant for the purpose and reads
the date he'd written on the inside
last time I was there. He asks me
my age. He's asked it before
but asks again. He's seven years older
and is pleased by the thought.
He changes the button cell, rubs out
the old date and puts in the new one.
With a watchmaker's brush he
cleans the groove and, clicking
the back case into position,
turns over the watch to set the time,
looking at the one on his wrist to set it.
Holding the strap from either end
as if making a gift, he hands me
the watch as all five grandfather clocks
strike 12 noon somewhat angrily.

Traffic Light at Waterworks

Sitting by a traffic light under the sea,
her white head bent,
how does she who's never spoken
tell the fish-headed men

that only lures at heavy discount,
as they always were,
are in the mall inside the clock tower
towards which they're rushing.

Laugh Club of Gandhi Park

In lanes too narrow
for three to walk abreast,
that only peddlers

with goods to sell
from upright bicycles enter,
are modest houses,

modest only in name,
behind whose barred windows,
ornamental gates,

the spikes along the top
painted black and gold,
live family men who can

wiggle their fiery
bellies at will.
You see them

in Gandhi Park,
on opposite benches,
practising their skills,

a smokescreen
of laughter
hiding their faces.

They move in a pack
and eat sprouts
on the way out.

Mistimed
badminton shots
exploding around him,

a metal soldier
with assault rifle
stands guard

and a musical fountain
plays fountain music
in the background.

Shelter

Park Bench

A colourless blue backpack,
the same that children
in kindergarten carry,
and a long umbrella-shaped
object wrapped in newspaper
looked like his only possessions.
He was busy rolling something.
Another time he was examining
a small plastic bag
thick with folded papers,
taking one out, putting one back.
Morning walkers whizzed past him
like wind-up cars. A few walked
in groups, taking up most
of the walking path, talking breathlessly.

Tent

Inches from me,
in a corner of the window sill,
its wood old and seasoned,
painted smoky grey
by my parents,
is a lightweight tent.
Pale white, it's covered
in dust. Ropes of unequal
length attach it to the sill.
When there's a storm
it blows over the tent.
The tent is open on all sides.
From the side nearest me,
which is also the widest,
a spider comes out and
steps back in again. I bend
my head to see where it's gone
but I cannot see all the way
inside, even though the tent
is the size of my thumbnail.
When the sun falls on them,
the tent ropes shine as though
made of ultra thin plastic wire.

Cage

It has slate grey fur,
matching button ears,
pointed pink-tipped nose,
a long tail.

I've been seeing it
occasionally,
beside a table,
running along a wall.

When I open the cupboard,
the one with suitcases
on top, I'm afraid
it'll jump out.

I set up the rat trap
under the sideboard
and waited. A day passed.
Another. I forgot about it.

Surrounded by
bread crumbs,
it was sitting inside,
making no sound,

its tail caught
in the cage door.
I tried to read
its expression,

wanting to
reassure it,
to tell it
that all was well

and I'll soon bring
something for it to eat.
After lunch I thought
I'd go out

and release it
in the open somewhere.
The street was empty.
On one side

was a grassy ditch.
I released it in the grass
thinking it would
run away but it hobbled

towards the shops
and was run over.
I don't know how
it happened.

It was the middle
of the afternoon,
there was little traffic,
not all shops were open.

It would have felt
no pain. Its tail
was the only thing left
that was recognisable.

Its last meal was
an arrowroot biscuit
I'd slipped through
the wire mesh.

Acknowledgements

Grateful acknowledgement is made to the editors of the following journals and anthologies where some of these poems first appeared: *India at 75* (PEN.org, 2022), *Literary Activism*, and *Poetry* (Chicago).

The Rahim *dohas* were published as a foldout booklet by Longhouse, and *Ghalib, A Diary* was published as a pamphlet by New Walk Editions. Thanks to Bob and Susan Arnold of Longhouse and Rory Waterman and Nick Everett of New Walk for making them possible.

My gratitude to Forrest Gander for reading through the Rahim *dohas* and for a suggestion that was quickly incorporated.

OTHER TITLES IN THE LITERARY ACTIVISM SERIES

On Being Indian by Amit Chaudhuri